TRADING
AND INVESTING
MADE EASY

Learn the basic foundations of how to be a successful trader and investor in the financial markets

DR ADEREMI BANJOKO

Co-author in the best selling *Wake Up... Live the Life You Love* book series

TRADING
AND INVESTING
MADE EASY

Learn the basic foundations of how
to be a successful trader and investor
in the financial markets

MakeWay
...making way for your ultimate success...

dkbMARKETS

All bible scriptures quoted are from the New King James Version (NKJV).

ISBN: 978-1-907925-48-1

TRADING AND INVESTING MADE EASY
Learn the basic foundations of how to be a successful trader and investor in the financial markets
is published by:
MakeWay Publishing Limited

www.makewaygroup.com

For orders and more information, please contact:
dKB Markets
Canton Concourse, 12 Landbridge Avenue
Oniru Estate, Victoria Island
Lagos, Nigeria
Email: info@dkbmarkets.com

www.dkbmarkets.com www.facebook.com/dkbmarkets
www.twitter.com/dkbmarkets www.youtube.com/dkbmarkets

This book may be purchased for educational, business, or sales promotional use.

Due to the author's background as an obstetrician and gynaecologist as well as his heart for orphans and widows, he has been actively involved in helping to improve maternal healthcare in Nigeria and supporting orphans and widows in Rwanda. To this end, a percentage of the proceeds from the sale of this book will go to **The Ark Foundation** (www.thearkfoundationng.org) that works to improve maternal healthcare in Nigeria and **Solace Ministries** (www.solacem.org / www.solaceministriesuk.com), which is involved in improving the lives of orphans and widows in Rwanda.

CONTENTS

PREFACE

I have always loved learning about different ways to create wealth. Straight out of medical school, I bought my first investment property in 1994 and I have not looked back since.

Along the way, I discovered the **financial markets** and found them both very interesting and fascinating. I loved the fact that it was a level playing field and anyone could get involved. I started trading and investing, read a lot of books and attended lots of seminars. During this period, I discovered (after many huge losses) that there were certain basic rules to trading and investing. Applying these rules to my **trading** and **investing** significantly improved my success.

I started to teach colleagues, friends and family on how to apply these rules; this led to me running seminars and courses on trading and investing in the financial markets and now, to writing this book.

I hope this book will give the would-be trader and investor a good foundation for success in the financial markets.

ACKNOWLEDGMENTS

I wish to give all honour and glory to God for gifting me the ability to write this book and also, to endure the good and bad experiences I have had during my career.

INTRODUCTION

BENEFITS OF TRADING AND INVESTING IN THE FINANCIAL MARKETS

**If you can actually count your money,
then you are not really a rich man
J PAUL GETTY**

As a trader and investor in the financial markets, I have recognised many benefits in trading and investing. These are;

1. Being your own boss – you make your own decisions about which markets to trade or invest in and decide your own strategies.

2. You do not require any qualifications – although you do need to learn the basics of trading and investing which this book will provide. You do not need to have a university degree to become a trader or Investor. Continual self-education on the financial markets, trading and investing is essential.

3. You can start with as little as $500 (or naira equivalent) – start small and with a good strategy and good money management, you can slowly build up your investment.

4. Earn unlimited amounts of money – there is no limit to how much you can earn trading and investing in the financial markets.

5. Trade and invest from anywhere in the world, hence you are not restricted and can make money on the move. All you need is a laptop and internet access.

6. Everyone is equal in the financial markets – the markets respect no one and do not discriminate against anyone.

7. You can trade and invest in a variety of financial markets in different countries such as indices, foreign exchange, commodities, individual stocks or shares.

8. You decide when or when not to trade and invest, making you the master of your time.

9. You will gain a better understanding of the financial markets and the world economy.

These, along with other benefits, make me excited about being a trader and investor.

CHAPTER 1

UNDERSTANDING FINANCIAL MARKETS' TERMINOLOGY

Life isn't about finding yourself. Life is about creating yourself.
GEORGE BERNARD SHAW

To be successful in the financial markets, it is important to understand clearly certain basic terminologies such as;

1. Trading and investing
2. Financial markets
3. Investment risk

We will be discussing each of these important terms in this chapter.

1. The Difference between Trading and Investing
It is very important from the outset to understand that **trading** is significantly different from **investing**. Trading is *short-term* and investing is *long-term*. With trading, you are looking to achieve your profit target within 24 hours (*Day Trading*) or within a couple of weeks or months (*Swing Trading* or *Positional Trading*). With investing, you are looking at a term of at least 5 to 10 years.

Trading
Trading involves speculating on the financial markets for immediate or short-term gains. Trading offers an opportunity to create good cashflow as another stream of income, once you have developed your mind-set sufficiently and 'learned the rules of trading.' This will be discussed further in the upcoming chapters.

Investing
Investing should be part of a core plan for building wealth and I strongly believe **everyone** should be an investor. This involves

putting varying amounts of money on a regular basis into investment vehicles such as mutual funds, index funds, stock and shares, and bonds.

The magic of compound interest is realised by this kind of investing, which magnifies small amounts invested over a period of time. This money will be very useful towards medium to long term goals such as school fees, buying a house and retirement.

2. Financial Markets
The financial markets are composed largely of four separate markets. These are:
(i)   The Fixed Income Securities Market – these are mainly bonds and treasury bills (T-Bills)
(ii)   The Stock Market – this involves companies' stocks and shares listed on countries' major stock exchanges
(iii)   The Currency Market or Foreign Exchange (Forex) Market
(iv)   The Commodities Market – this involves commodities such as oil, gold, coffee and wheat

Although there are inter-relationships between these markets, each of them has its own peculiarities and they should be assessed on their own merit. Separating these markets is also helpful when it comes to assessing investment risk.

3. Investment Risk
Investment risk simply means your chances of *losing money*! Low risk means low chance of losing money, medium risk means a medium chance of losing money and high risk means a high chance of losing money. The financial markets can also be categorised according to risk – low, medium and high risk.

Low Risk

The best market for this is the *Fixed Income Securities Market* – bonds and T-Bills. As of the time of publication[1], the 10-year government bonds have annual return rates in the following countries shown below.

- 0.45% to 1.69% in the United Kingdom
- 10% to 15% in Nigeria

If you are risk averse and want to preserve your capital, then you are low risk and fall into this category.

Medium Risk

If you have some risk appetite and do not mind losing some money if that were to happen, then you can take medium risk. The best option will be *long-term investment* in the stock market. The following are stock market annual return rates in the United States of America[2]:

- 26.5% for the year ended December 31, 2013
- 8.48% for the year ended December 31, 2014
- -0.57% for the year ended December 31, 2015

High Risk

If you have a high risk appetite with the knowledge that you could potentially lose all your money then you fall into the high-risk category. The best market for this is **trading** the forex or commodities market – this has a potential of a 100%+ annual return rate.

As you can see, the higher the risk, the higher the returns.

---

[1] Source: http://www.tradingeconomics.com/bonds accessed at 10:45hrs GMT+1 on March 25, 2016
[2] Dow Jones Industrials (source): https://ycharts.com/indices/%5EDJI/ytd_return accessed at 10:48hrs GMT+1 on March 25, 2016

CHAPTER 2
TRADING BASICS

The greatest barrier to success is the fear of failure
SVEN GORAN

Trading offers an opportunity to create good cashflow once you have developed your mind-set sufficiently and learned the *rules of trading*. Remember, trading may involve heavy losses, which can be minimised with a strong development of your mind-set.

To become a successful trader in the financial market, you must possess what I call the *Three M's* – **M**ind, **M**oney Management and **M**ethod.

Mind (Trading Psychology)

A disciplined mind is an absolute requirement for successful trading. Managing to conquer the devils of **greed** and **fear** will enable you to become a successful trader. Greed could make you take unnecessary risks leading to **huge** losses. Fear may paralyse you and stop you from placing trades – this leads to losing out on potentially profitable trades.

Learn to manage your emotions. Your success or failure as a trader is largely due to your ability to control your emotions and maintain your discipline. ***Your goal should be to trade well and not to make money! If you trade well, you will make money.***

Money Management

This is another important factor in trading. The *first* goal of money management is *survival!* You need to avoid taking risks that could potentially wipe out your trading account capital. The *second* goal is to earn a steady return and the *third* is to continue to improve on the second goal.

Taking into consideration your capital investment, managing your risk per trade is extremely crucial to your success in becoming a profitable trader.

Method

There needs to be a plan or methodology to trading which is not based on tips, hunches, visions or dreams. Developing a personalised trading plan is essential; without which, you are setting yourself up for failure.

It is not only important to have a trading plan, you have to be disciplined and stick to it!

So, you need to remember that trading the correct way, with the *Three M's* in mind, will make you money. If your target is just to earn money instead of trading the proper way, this may lead to the loss of huge sums of money. The *Three M's* will be discussed in more detail in subsequent chapters.

Opening a Trading Account

It is now very easy to open a trading account.

It is very important, as a beginner, to have a mentor guide you through placing your first trades, setting up your trading platform and helping you with understanding how to analyse the financial markets.

Getting started and opening a trading account will be discussed in detail in Chapter 10.

dkbMARKETS provides a trading platform and also coaching and mentoring on how to be a successful trader. Details can be seen at www.dkbmarkets.com.

*Always remember, the financial markets are dynamic with real people buying and selling for various reasons which may be logical or illogical. Hence, the financial market does not follow what the textbooks or analysts say. Avoid using the words **always** and **never** when analysing the markets.*

CHAPTER 3

MIND (THE PSYCHOLOGY OF TRADING) AND MONEY MANAGEMENT

Knowing is not enough, we must apply. Willing is not enough, we must do.
GOETHE

Mind (Psychology of Trading)

This happens to be the most important aspect of trading. A large part of your success is down to you and your discipline! In order to be a successful trader, you need to master your mind and trading psychology.

Here are some guidelines to help you understand trading psychology.

1. **Learn to manage your emotions**

    You need to be objective and clear in your mind when assessing the financial markets. If you are upset, excited, tired, angry or distracted for any reason, you should not be trading until you have brought your emotions under control. Your feelings have an immediate impact on your trading account.

2. **Do not ignore change in mass psychology**

    The trend in the market is a reflection of what the majority of the traders in the market think. If the majority of traders in the market are buying, the market and trend will go up but if the majority of traders decide to sell, the direction of the market can change and start to trend downwards. This means you should be willing to change your mind once you notice a change in the direction of the market. Ignoring change in mass psychology can result in huge losses. It pays to remember the old saying *'The trend is your friend.'*

You need to be humble as a trader and be willing to change your mind and cut your losses. Huge losses may occur if you become arrogant and refuse to change your mind when the markets are moving against you.

3. Trade less often

Every trade you place is a potentially losing trade, hence the more trades you place the greater the risk of losing a lot of money. Usually the biggest mistake new traders make is to think the more trades they place, the more successful they will be.

4. Trading is deceptively easy

Being successful in your first few trades can lead to the notion that trading is easy. Huge losses may result because the trader can become over confident, greedy, and not aware of the other factors that come into play with trading such as money management, fundamental analysis, economic news, chart patterns and the previous history of the market.

5. The goal is to trade well and not to make money

If you trade well, you will make money. My advice to new traders is to focus on how to properly analyse the financial markets; formulate a trading plan; develop their mind; good discipline; and apply good money management to their trades. Focusing solely on profits and making money leads to poor decision-making, greed, overtrading, poor money management and lack of discipline; this may all lead to huge losses.

6. You are responsible for your trades

Learning to take responsibility for your trades will help you learn from your bad trades and help improve your trading. Blaming the news, friends, your broker, your mentor or anyone and anything around you for your bad trades will prevent you learning from these bad trades and render you doomed to repeating the same mistakes. It is also a good idea to keep a diary of your trades. Continuous analysis of your trades and yourself aids the development of a successful trading career. Importantly, keep reading, attending seminars and learning about the financial markets and trading.

7. Beware there are enormous temptations in the market

The markets can be highly volatile with sudden changes in direction. Without a good trading plan and discipline, this could lead to emotionally driven trades resulting in huge losses.

8. Rags to riches and riches to rags stories

Applying the basics of trading well, (the *Three M's*), could create a rags to riches story. Indiscipline, failure to plan and not applying the *Three M's* could lead to riches to rags stories.

9. Formulate a trading plan

Write down your trading plan and stick to it. Plan your trades and trade your plan! See Chapter 6 on Your Trading Plan.

10. Strict Money Management rules

This is the subject of discussion in the next section.

Money Management

This is the most critical, yet frequently overlooked, aspect associated with trading. Irrespective of which financial market(s) you are trading, what trading programme or strategy an individual is using or whether the market is up or down, without excellent money management, you will not succeed in turning out to be a profitable trader.

Using excellent money management, you can end up being a profitable trader with a winning percentage of less than 50 per cent of your trades. In a good article written by Dr Van K Tharp[3], he states that,

> Most of us grew up exposed to an educational system that brainwashes us with the idea that you have to get 94-95% correct to be excellent. And if you can't get at least 70% correct you're a failure. Mistakes are severely punished in the school system by ridicule and poor grades, yet it is only through mistakes that human beings learn. Contrast that with the real world in which a .300 hitter in baseball gets paid millions. In fact, in the everyday world few people are close to perfect and most of us who do well are probably right less than half the time. Indeed, people have made millions on trading systems with reliabilities around 40%.

What this means in a simplistic way is that, every time you trade, regardless of your trading strategy, that trade has a 60 per cent chance of being a losing trade and a 40 per cent chance of being a successful trade. This means that there are more chances of your trades being losing trades than successful trades and hence, trading is not for the risk averse. This also shows that greed can lead to huge losses. With proper money management and discipline, you can still be an overall profitable trader.

[3.] Dr Van K Tharp: **Why It's so Difficult for Most People to Make Money in the Market** (Market Technicians Association, November 1997 newsletter edition)

Gerald Loeb[4] wrote as follows:

> The most important single thing I learned is that accepting losses promptly is the first key to success…

> The difference between the investor who year in and year out procures for himself a final net profit and the one who is usually in the red is not entirely a question of superior selection of stocks or superior timing. Rather, it is also a case of **knowing how to capitalise on successes and curtail failures**.

Your ultimate objective of accomplishing profitability will remain out of reach if good care is not actually taken in order to control the amount of capital allocated to each position, as even wildly successful traders are not invulnerable to a string of losing positions.

Goals of money management are ranked as follows:

1. *Long-term survival* – You want to survive each day with enough capital left in your account to trade the following day.
2. *Steady growth of your capital by trading with discipline and good money management* – By doing this, you can gradually increase your risk as your capital increases which leads to the third priority.
3. *High profits* – Winners think, feel and act differently from losers. You might have to change your personality.

---

[4] Gerald M Loeb: **The Battle for Investment Survival** (Wilder Publications, 2010)

Tips for Successful Trading

1. Decide you are in the market for the long haul, namely, 20+ years. This is not a *get-rich-quick* scheme. Focus on managing your risks and not on your profits. Learn to live to trade another day by not taking undue risks and jeopardising your entire capital in one day!

2. Learn as much as you can from books, seminars, and experts, but be sceptical. Continual education is very important in becoming a good trader.

3. Do not get greedy and rush to trade – learn to trade properly.

4. Develop a method of analysing the market.

5. Be aware, traders could be the weakest link in trading.

CHAPTER 4

FUNDAMENTAL ANALYSIS AND INTER-MARKET ANALYSIS

It is hard to fail, but it is worse never to
have tried to succeed
THEODORE ROOSEVELT

FUNDAMENTAL ANALYSIS (FA)

Definition: This is the examination involving any main factors which influence the state of a country's economy, industry groups and companies.

The goal is usually to derive a prediction and then benefit from future price movements. FA is actually performed on three levels, as stated in the definition, starting typically through the country's economic level, then the industry sector level as well as finally, the company level.

Country's National Economy Stage

When analysing a country's economy, you should focus on economic data to analyse the existing as well as long-term growth of that particular economy. Whenever the economy grows, industry groups and companies benefit and also expand. When the overall economy shrinks or declines, most sectors as well as companies are affected.

Generally, there are several economic data to be aware of, which impact the economy such as interest rates, Gross Domestic Product (GDP), consumer price index and unemployment figures to name but a few.

Industry Stage

This involves the examination of the actual supply and demand forces pertaining to the products and services of the industry sector you are interested in.

Generally, you identify industry sectors which usually profit the most out of growth of the economy and the industry sectors that are usually affected the least from the downfall associated with the economy. It is much more beneficial to choose to be in the right industry sector than selecting the correct stock. You will need to search to find the *leaders* and *innovators* within the industry group.

Company Stage
This requires you to actually assess the financial data, management, organisation concept as well as levels of competition relating to the company you are interested in.

Deriving current good value and forecasting foreseeable future stock prices requires analysis involving all three levels.

Advantages of Fundamental Analysis include:

> ➤ A good decision making tool for long-term investments based on long-term trends

> ➤ The identification of valuable stocks

> ➤ A development of a thorough understanding of the business

Disadvantages of Fundamental Analysis are:

> ➤ Time constraints – to adequately and fundamentally analyse the markets consumes time; hence, this is more essential for investors rather than traders.

> ➤ It is heavily based on subjectivity – a fair value of a stock is based on assumptions

> ➤ Analyst bias – the majority of the information that goes into the analysis comes from the company itself

INTER-MARKET ANALYSIS

Structural shifts involving economic markets have arisen because the global economy has emerged due to innovations within telecommunications as well as escalating internationalisation associated with business and commerce. Hardly any economy will be isolated in the current world financial system. It is important to factor into your analysis, outside inter-market forces that impact each market traded.

Inter-market analysis examines the correlations between the four major parts of the financial markets: stocks, fixed income securities (bonds and T-Bills), commodities and currencies (forex).

Most of the commodities' industry carries an impact on the treasury notes and bonds. This has a strong impact on the equities market, which in turn influences the price of the United States dollar as well as foreign exchange markets, which subsequently has an effect on commodities; and the cycle continues.

In addition, the United States economy can influence the world's market segments and the world's markets present an impact on the American economy. Investors and traders can use these relationships to identify opportunities in the markets and improve their analyses of the markets.

The inter-market relationships depend on the forces of inflation or deflation. In a "normal" inflationary environment, stocks and bonds are positively correlated. This means they both move in the same direction.

These are the key inter-market relationships in an inflationary environment:

- A *positive* relationship between bonds and stocks. Bonds usually change direction ahead of stocks

- An *inverse* relationship between bonds and commodities

- An *inverse* relationship between the United States dollar and commodities

- Interest rates rise when bonds fall. In an inflationary environment, stocks react positively to falling interest rates (rising bond prices). Low interest rates stimulate economic activity and boost corporate profits.

In a deflationary environment when stocks are *down*, commodities are also *down*, dollar goes *up* and bonds are *up*. When stocks are *up*, commodities are also *up*, dollar goes *down* and bonds are *down*. Stocks and bonds have an inverse relationship. This also means that stocks have a positive relationship with interest rates.

While these inter-market relationships generally work over longer periods of time, they are subject to periods when the relationships do not work.

Other Examples of Inter-Market Analysis

Gold, Oil and Foreign Exchange

If the actual worth of the United States dollar drops, gold prices rise – the United States dollar and gold usually go in opposite directions.

You can find some sort of positive correlation between the Euro and gold. The actual value associated with the euro and gold prices frequently move in the same direction.

Oil is currently an important commodity driving worldwide economic growth. Oil prices and foreign exchange possess an important association in the global economy. Raised oil prices weaken the yen and strengthen the value of the pound sterling.

Agricultural Commodities

Exports associated with agricultural commodities account for a sizable portion of American farm revenue.

- Whenever the value of the dollar rises, this cuts down interest coming from importing nations because of the commodity's inflated costs; as a result there is a fall within the commodity market.

- If the value of the dollar drops, commodity prices become cheap and the market goes up.

*Always remember, the financial markets are dynamic with real people buying and selling for various reasons which may be logical or illogical. Hence the financial markets do not always follow what the textbooks or analysts say. Avoid using the words **ALWAYS** and **NEVER** when analysing the markets.*

CHAPTER 5

TECHNICAL ANALYSIS AND INDICATORS

Energy and persistence conquer all things
BENJAMIN FRANKLIN

Various definitions of Technical Analysis describe it as:

- A technique of reviewing market activity (commodities, forex, stocks and shares and indices) patterns on any graph and/or chart in order to discover buying and selling possibilities.

- A visual representation of price and volume movements through a timeframe

- The predicting of market prices through methods of study from information created through the course of trading. For example, while trading a particular market, you might notice price patterns indicating a rise in the market price giving you an indication on when to trade.

Technical analysis is not only effective for the short-term or medium-term trader; it also aids the long-term investor.

In order to be a good trader, knowledge of how to examine a trading chart is crucial. Failure to assess, figure out and interpret the charts of the markets you are trading makes you sorely handicapped. Reading books in addition to articles on technical analysis and continual education is very important to becoming a successful trader.

Technical analysis will *not* predict the foreseeable future; however, it will provide a guide to analyse the market and come up with reasonable options to trade.

One of the most important goals associated with graph and/or chart study is to verify the trend associated with the market. As previously stated, a very good old and popular statement within trading the financial markets is that *the trend is your* friend. The trend is the observable course associated with the market which could be up, down or sideways. Trading in the direction associated with the trend can substantially boost your chances of success.

Indicators

This means any kind of numerical calculation that is displayed graphically upon the graph and/or chart, other than *time* and *price*. Indicators facilitate the analysis of the markets. Be very careful not to make use of too many indicators on your graph or chart as this could lead to confusion, which may even hamper your trading. It is plausible to use two indicators, or a maximum of three, on a chart. Indicators are mainly used to decide entry and exit points in the markets.

Types of Indicators

There are many indicators used in trading and it is outside the scope of this book to explain all the different indicators and how to use them. A few examples of how to use them can be found in Chapter 8 on Trading Strategies. I recommend you read up and study the individual indicators you choose to trade with.

A few of the frequently used indicators are;

➢ Candlesticks

➢ Trend Lines

➢ Support and Resistance

- Moving Averages (MA)
- Pivot Points
- Volume
- Fibonacci Retracement
- MACD – Moving Average Convergence Divergence

CHAPTER 6

METHOD OF TRADING - YOUR TRADING PLAN

Only through experiences of trial and suffering can the soul be strengthened
HELEN KELLER

Here are Four Important Reasons to have a Trading Plan

1. A *trading plan* helps you design your trades – adopting a method or strategy is very important; otherwise, frankly speaking, you are gambling and not trading.

2. It makes you consistent – having a plan minimises guesswork and improves consistency in your trades. This helps you become a successful trader.

3. Objectivity – having a plan enhances the analysis of your trading strategy and trading history in an objective way because you have been applying a consistent plan. This aids your assessment in an objective way whether your plan is successful or not.

4. To establish discipline – this is a way of keeping yourself in check and avoiding outside interference with your trading. It is also a way of assessing yourself as to whether *you* (perhaps your feelings and emotions) are the cause of your bad trades or the plan (checks if you are applying the *Three M's* to your trading).

A trading method or strategy, consistency, objectivity and discipline make the components of a good trader.

Simple features of a trading plan should;

➢ State which markets you wish to trade
➢ State which timeframe in which you wish to trade for the chosen market
➢ Have strict criteria for market entry – identifying which indicators to use
➢ Set strict criteria for market exit – when profit target has been reached and more importantly, when loss limit has also been reached to exit market. *This is where money management comes into effect.*

Example of a Simple Trading Plan (for illustration purposes only)

➢ Market to Trade – will trade the forex market, specifically the EUR/USD currency pair
➢ Trade Volume Size – will trade 0.1 *vol* which is $1 per pip[5] on the dkbMARKETS trading platform
➢ Use **Risk** (how many pips you are willing to lose if the market goes against you) to **Reward** (how many pips you plan to make if the market moves in your direction) ratio of 1:3 (*Day Trading*)
➢ Use a **Stop Loss** (set a limit of how many pips you are willing to lose if the market goes against you) of 20 pips and *profit limit* (set a limit of how many pips you want to make if the market moves in your direction) of 60 pips (*Day Trading*)
➢ Always check the economic calendar for reports of *high* importance before you commence trading for the day
➢ Do not trade prior to the release of a report of high importance

---

[5] PIP – Percentage In Points (used to measure forex market increments)

- Check the 1-year daily chart first for an overview of the market and for *Swing Trading* opportunities
- For *Swing Trades* (see Chapter 7), use the **Moving Averages** to determine entry and exit points
- For *Day Trading*, – use the *2-days 5-minute* chart and *pivot points* indicator for points of entry into the market
- Use the *Moving Average 50* (MA50) as the trend indicator and only trade in the direction of the trend
- When the market is trending sideways, *do not trade!*
- When I have 3 consecutive losses, *I stop trading for the day!*
- When profit target has been achieved, *I stop trading for the day!*

CHAPTER 7

SWING TRADING

If you don't start somewhere you will get nowhere
BOB MARLEY

There is a huge difference between trading and investing. Whereas a trader is looking for short-term gains in one day to a couple of months; an investor is looking for long-term gains, five to ten years or more.

A Trader can be a *Day Trader*, a *Swing Trader* or both.

A Day Trader is looking to achieve profit targets within 24 hours whilst a Swing Trader is looking to achieve profit targets within a few days or sometimes over several weeks. Swing trading is sometimes also called Position Trading. *Options Trading* is a form of swing trading.

Four Important Points for Swing Trading
1.   As a swing trader, you must have discipline and patience to wait until your profit target is reached
2.   You trade in the direction of the trend and wait for clear opportunities to catch the trend
3.   You must have very good money management
4.   You must have a trading plan to define clearly your entry and exit criteria into the market

Benefits of Swing Trading
1.   You trade less often; hence, reduced risk
2.   You do not have to constantly watch the market
3.   Your decisions are made when the markets are quiet or at the end of the trading day when analysis is less stressful
4.   Due to the above benefits, you are able to fit in Swing Trading with your other work commitments

CHAPTER 8
TRADING STRATEGIES

Failure is the opportunity to begin again more intelligently
HENRY FORD

Trading strategies are an important aspect of your trading plan. This involves deciding when to trade:

- when *not* to trade
- what criteria and indicators you will use to determine your entry point into the market
- an exit strategy
- a decision to use *Swing Trading* or *Day Trading*

When assessing the market in which you wish to trade, the first thing you want to do is determine the trend of the market. A trend is the discernible direction of the market. The markets can trend three ways:

1. Up-trader looking to *buy* – Up-trending market makes *higher highs* and *higher lows*.

2. Down-trader looking to *sell* – Down-trending market makes *lower lows* and *lower highs*

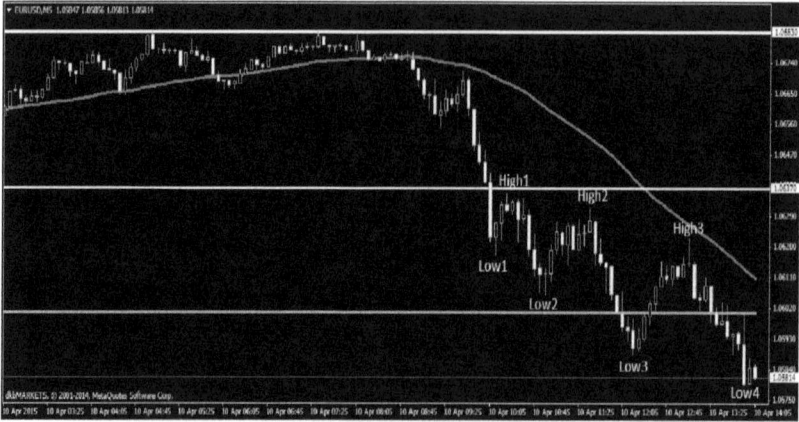

3. *Sideways* – trader keeps out of the market

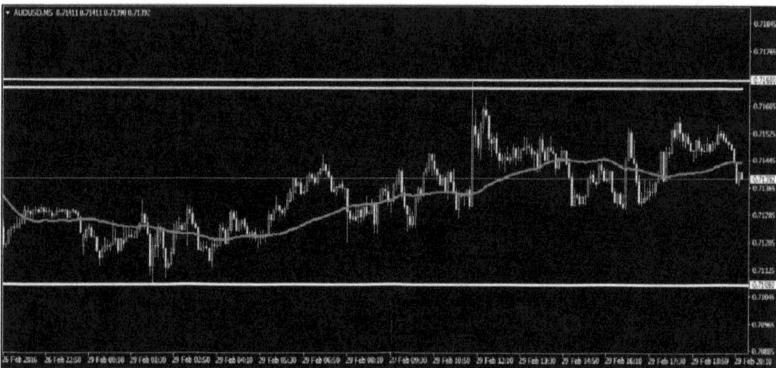

Sideways Trend – When to Avoid Trading

Markets tend to trend sideways under certain conditions – the words, *always* and *never*, do not exist in the markets. Anything can happen in the markets at any time and for no logical reason!

There are three major scenarios that could cause the markets to trend sideways.

1.   **Uncertainty in the Markets**

When there is uncertainty in the financial markets and traders are not sure what the outcome will be, the markets tend to trend sideways until there is certainty to the outcome.

Some examples are:

- The period leading up to major elections in the United Kingdom (prime ministerial and parliamentary elections) and the United States of America (presidential elections). This is because the United Kingdom is the financial capital of the world and the United States of America is the largest economy on the globe.
- Immediately prior to the release of the latest economic reports of *high* importance of the day.

2. **Reduced Volume of Traders**

When there are few traders in the markets, the markets tend to trend sideways. Some examples are:

- Public Holidays in the United Kingdom and the United States of America.
- Between 9:00pm and midnight GMT+1 – during this time period, all stock exchanges around the world are closed hence, there will be a reduced number of traders in the markets and the markets tend to trend sideways.

3. **Day after *huge* moves (100 – 120 pips) in the market**

When a market experiences a huge move in a day, that market tends to trend sideways on the following day.

In summary…

-   Have a clearly written down *trading plan*
-   Decide when and when *not* to trade
-   Decide which technical indicators to use
-   Define clearly your entry and exit criteria
-   Stick to your plan and be consistent!

There are as many strategies as there are traders that can be used for Swing Trading and Day Trading. It is advisable to attend seminars and lectures on trading and also seek the guidance of a mentor on how to use these or other strategies in trading and most importantly, to help you formulate your own trading strategy.

*It is very important to remember that a trading strategy with a 100 per cent success rate **does not exist**!* It will be a futile attempt to look for the perfect trading strategy. You can be a very successful trader with a winning percentage of 40 per cent of trades (see Chapter 3 on Money Management).

A few simple examples of trading strategies that I use:
Swing Trading
Using the **Moving Averages (MA)** – MA50 (black line) and MA30 (red line) on the *1 year daily* chart timeframe as entry and exit points. See chart below.

Here are a few simple examples of trading strategies I use.

Swing Trading
- Using the **Moving Averages (MA)** - Ma50 (Black line) & Ma30 (Red line) on the 1year Daily chart time frame - As entry and exit points. See chart below.

38

Day Trading

- Using *pivot points* (broken horizontal lines) on the *2-day 5 minutes* chart timeframe as entry and exit points (see chart below).

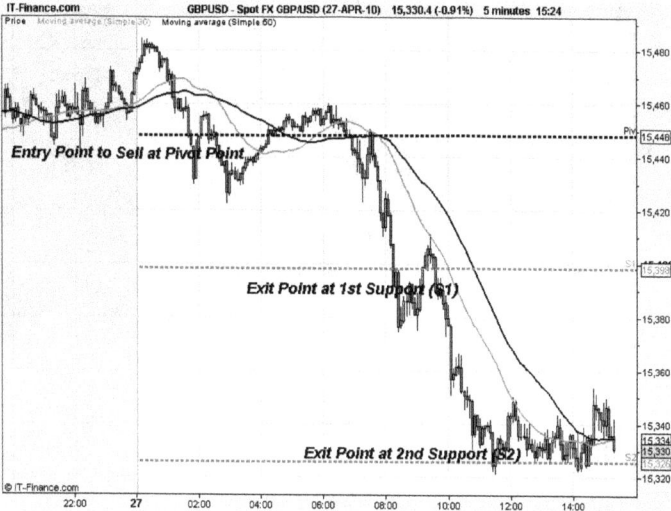

- **Support and Resistance** – Identifying the *support* and *resistance* levels in the markets and trading the breakouts from a sideways trend (see chart below).

CHAPTER 9
MARKETS TO TRADE

**After climbing a great hill, one only finds that there
are many more hills to climb
NELSON MANDELA**

Another trading plan consideration is the markets you trade. There are lots of different markets with sufficient liquidity to allow prudent speculation. However, it is important to select markets that are appropriate for your account size, risk level and trading style.

If you trade a diversified portfolio, there is a greater chance that you will catch some of the truly big moves that make for successful trading.

The financial markets consist of different types of markets you can trade such as stock market indices, foreign exchange (forex), individual stocks, and the commodities market.

Stock Market Index/Indices

A stock market index is a method of measuring a stock market as a whole. The most regularly quoted market indices are broad-based ones comprising the stocks of large companies listed on a nation's largest stock exchange, such as:

- The British FTSE 100
- The American DJ 30 and S&P 500 (respectively, the *Dow Jones* and *Small and Poor*)
- The German DAX 30
- The Australian Aussie 200
- The French CAC 40

Index Weighting

They involve the total market capitalisation of the firms weighted by their effect on the index, so that the bigger stocks would make more of a difference to the index in comparison to a smaller market capitalised company.

Price-Weighted Index – such as the FTSE, the cost of each component stock is the sole consideration when determining the value of the index.

Market Value-Weighted or Capitalisation-Weighted Index – like the Hang Seng Index, it factors in the size of the company.

Innovative techniques of index construction will supplant traditional market capitalisation-weighted indices as the dominant driver of equity baselines within 20 years, according to the FTSE Group.

Market Cap Indices Face New Rivals

A number of alternative approaches have emerged lately, such as fundamental indices in which stocks are weighted by metrics like book value, dividends and sales and minimum variance, in which portfolios are designed to reduce volatility.

The FTSE has recently launched a family of Risk Efficient Indices. This covers the United States of America, the United Kingdom, the Euro zone, Japan and the Asia-Pacific zone and has outperformed standard indices in back-testing. Legal and General Investment Management runs just £800 million of passive money base-lined to fundamental indices, compared with about £150 billion linked to market capitalisation.
This shows strong support for the traditional market capitalisation index.

FTSE (The Financial Times Stock (London) Exchange)

This is a share index of the 100 most highly capitalised United Kingdom firms noted on the London Stock Exchange. The index began on January 3, 1984 with a base level of 1,000 (one thousand); the highest worth reached to date is 6950.6 on December 30, 1999.

The index is maintained by the FTSE Group, an independent company which originated as collaboration between *The Financial Times* and the *London Stock Exchange*. It is figured out in real-time and published every 15 seconds.

The FTSE 100 companies represent about 81 per cent of the market capitalisation of the entire London Stock Exchange. Although the FTSE All-Share Index is more comprehensive, the FTSE 100 is by far the most generally used United Kingdom stock market indicator.

As of September 30, 2008, the net market capitalisation of the FTSE 100 Index was £1,171 billion.

Things That Affect Indices

- Economic data such as the gross domestic product, consumer price index, unemployment rate and interest rates
- Company data and earnings release
- Time of the year – buy in November and sell in April

Stock Market Exchange Approximate Opening Times (GMT+0 times)

- FTSE 100   8:00am – 4:30pm
- Dow Jones   2.30pm – 9:00pm
- DAX 30   7:00am – 9:00pm
- Aussie 200   10:50pm – 5:30am

Foreign Exchange Market – (FX or Forex)

The foreign exchange market is the largest and most liquid of the world's financial markets. More than $2 trillion is traded daily in the FX market. It is a 24-hour market.

Advantages of FX Trading

- Diversification
- Global market
- 24-hour trading
- Electronic trading
- Liquidity
- Leverage
- Simplicity
- Good technical market
- Not too volatile

Background of FX Trading

Following the *Bretton Woods Agreement* (1944-1971), the US dollar was fixed to gold at a price of $35 an ounce. Richard Nixon[6], however, on August 15, 1971, removed the United

---

[6.] Richard Milhous Nixon – the 37th President of the United States of America (1969 to 1974) who became the only US President to date, to resign the office.

States of America from the "gold standard". This led to the *Smithsonian Agreement* in December 1971. With this and the advent of computers, technology and the internet, the FX market blossomed to what it is today.

There is no central exchange for the FX market. It functions through a global network of banks, corporations and individuals trading one currency for another. The FX market was initially developed to facilitate trade between countries. Today, a large part of the FX market is traded on speculation, arbitrage and professional dealing.

Currency Pair

The FX is a 2-dimensional product. It is quoted as the price of one currency against another. The base currency is always quoted first and this has a constant of 1. The base currency is what you are buying or selling.

For example, with a quote like this, **EUR/USD 1.2619**, the euro is quoted first; hence, it has a constant of 1 and it is the euro that you will be buying or selling. This quote will be interpreted as 1 EUR will buy 1.2619 USD.

PIPs

FX market increments are measured in PIPs which means Percentage in Points (PIPs). A pip is the fourth digit from the decimal point for all currency pairs except for currency pairs which consist of the Japanese yen where a pip is the second digit after the decimal point. The following are examples:

- EUR/USD 1.4127 – for all currency pairs (except where the yen is in the pair), you start counting your pips from the fourth digit after the decimal point.

- USD/JPY 80.88 – once you have the yen in the currency pair, you start counting your pips from the second digit after the decimal point.

Factors that affect the FX Market

- Economic data such as unemployment rate, interest rate decisions, gross domestic product (GDP) and consumer price index (CPI) to name but a few
- Major events in the financial markets such as the housing crisis in the United States of America, the Greek/Euro crisis or oil prices could also affect the FX market.

Individual Stocks

There are 3,041 securities (stocks) traded in the United Kingdom and 262 securities in Nigeria as of the time of writing. Assessing stocks involves fundamental analysis, which is the examination of the financial data, management, business concept and competition of the company. *Technical Analysis* is also very important in assessing stocks.

Ways of Trading and Investing in Stocks

- Buy for long-term investment
- Short-term trading (long or short)
- Buying a portfolio of stocks and hedging

Commodities Market

There are various markets you can trade within the commodities market.

- In the energy complex, crude oil, heating oil and natural gas are good trading vehicles
- In the food sector, coffee, orange juice and sugar are recommended
- In metals, you can trade gold, silver and copper
- In the agricultural sector, corn, oats, soya beans and cotton are the best

CHAPTER 10

GETTING STARTED AND OPENING A TRADING ACCOUNT

**The soul of a lazy man desires and has nothing;
but the soul of the diligent shall be rich
PROVERBS 13:4[7]**

It is important to have coaching and mentoring when you first start to trade in order to avoid expensive mistakes. You should choose a broker who, amongst other things, offers coaching and mentoring as part of their services.

dkbMARKETS offers this and more to traders. dkbMARKETS is run by highly experienced industry professionals bringing you first class service. They assist you in becoming a successful trader in the financial markets. Regular live and online seminars, workshops and master classes are run by dkbMARKETS.

For *live account holders*, dkbMARKETS also runs weekly live trading webinars which enables our live account holders to ask questions regarding trading, the platform or any issues they might have related to trading.

To open a *live trading account* today, go to www.dkbmarkets.com. You can also open a demo account to practise trading. You will need to scan and submit the following documentation for you to complete your *live trading account* registration process and activate your account:

- You will need one proof of identification
- One proof of residential address that must contain your name and address

---

[7] New King James version

CHAPTER 11

LONG-TERM INVESTMENT IN THE FINANCIAL MARKETS

Always bear in mind that your own resolution to success is more important than any other one thing
ABRAHAM LINCOLN

What is the Foundation of Long-Term Investing?
To emerge as a successful long term investor, you need to develop these four crucial financial skills:
1.   How to appreciate the value of money
2.   How to control money
3.   Actively implement effective ways to save money
4.   And finally, ways to invest money

How to appreciate the value of money
Investing just $30 (or its naira equivalent) a month can generate a million dollars ($1million) by way of the influence of compound interest. The dictionary definition of compound interest is:

> Interest paid on both the principal (capital) and on accrued interest.

Wealthy individuals *gain* compound interest while poor individuals *pay* compound interest.

During my early years in business, I often had more credit cards and personal loan debts than income from my businesses. I soon realised that despite payments to loan companies, the outstanding debt was more or less the same. It is important to make your money work for you than you work for money! I started looking for investments and businesses that earned me compound interest and became mindful of what I spent my money on.

Using a compound interest calculator, below is a table showing how long it will take to generate a million dollars on saving $30 (or naira equivalent) per month, depending on the interest rate.

Interest Rate	Time (in years) to generate $1million by saving $30 per month
5%	101
10%	59
15%	43
20%	35

There are different ways to look at this table. First and foremost, you need to find the money to invest. If you want to shorten the duration, you will need to invest more. Think about what you are currently spending your money on and whether you are spending wisely and investing wisely.

The other point to note from this table is the importance of starting early when it comes to investing for your children's future.

How to Control and Save Money
It is very important to record all your income and expenses. Poor recordkeeping of my income and expenses was a major reason for my earlier failures in business. With a very clear view of your financial situation, you will be able to see where you are losing money and where you might save money.

Once you have a clear picture of your finances, save at least 6 to 9 months of emergency money in order for you to cover your expenses for that period in the event of job loss or collapse of business. From then on, 50 per cent from your savings go straight to your long-term investment account.

See Appendix 1 for an example of a simple income and expenses spreadsheet you can use.

Long-Term Investment
This enables investors to gain from wealth generation and the growth associated with a nation's economy. This is done by finding a way to invest in the stock market of a country you are interested in. Hence, the first decision to make in long-term investing is which country *you think* is going to generate wealth and economic growth in the next 10 to 20 years.

You can choose to invest in *stocks and shares*, *mutual funds*, *index fu*nds, *exchange traded funds* (ETFs), *cash*, *bonds* and so on, in the country of your choice. You do not necessarily need to learn everything regarding these types of passive financial instruments, but you should be aware of the essential basics.

The Basics of Long-Term Investing
There are three main methods for investors to gain access to the stock market.

1. **Invest directly in Fixed Income Securities (Bonds and T-bills) and Stocks and Shares**
   There are more than 262 stocks to choose from in Nigeria alone and much more if you are looking to invest in other

countries. This form of investment requires a good knowledge of the company you are interested in. You should get to know the products or services of the company, the competition, future plans, management board and other relevant details of the company. You also have to know how to read company financials and understand price/earnings[8] (P/E) ratios, earnings per share[9] (EPS) and other terms involved in the understanding of these financial reports.

All this is time consuming but good knowledge and experience will provide you with the ability to pick good stocks. A full and comprehensive discussion on how to pick good stocks to invest in long term is outside the scope of this book and this is a method of long-term investing that beginners will need to approach with extreme caution.

Warren Buffett is the greatest stock picker in the world.

2. **Investments in Actively Managed Funds – Mutual Funds**
   A **mutual fund** is a professionally managed type of collective investment scheme that pools money from many investors and invests in stocks and shares and other financial instruments. The mutual fund will have a fund manager who buys and sells the fund's investments in accordance with the fund's investment objective.

   There are mutual funds that invest in stocks and shares of companies; these are called *Equity Funds*. Mutual funds that invest in bonds are called *Fixed-Income Funds* and those that invest in the money market are known as a *Money Market Fund*.

---

[8] Price/Earnings Ratio – a valuation ratio of a company's current share price compared to its per-share earnings
[9] Earnings per Share – the portion of a company's profit allocated to each outstanding share of common stock

Basically, you are getting someone else to pick the companies and stocks on your behalf in exchange for a management fee payment.

The benchmark for most mutual funds is the index of the country where the fund is invested. A nation's index represents the performance of the stock market of a given nation and this usually reflects investor sentiment on the state of its economy. The index in Nigeria is called the All Share Index. In the United States of America, the index is the Dow Jones 30 (top 30 companies) or the Standard & Poor (S&P) 500 (the top 500 companies). In the United Kingdom, it is called the FTSE 100, which comprises the top 100 largest capitalised companies in that country.

Many fund managers attempt to achieve better returns than the returns of the index of the country they are based in and are largely unsuccessful.

3. Invest in Passively Managed Funds
Index funds and *Exchange Traded Funds* are passively managed funds as explained below.

An Index Fund is a portfolio constructed to match or track the components of a market index, such as the FTSE 100 in the United Kingdom or the Standard & Poor's 500 Index (S&P 500) in the United States of America. An index fund provides broad market exposure, hence, spreading and reducing the risk.

An Exchange Traded Fund (ETF) is a security that tracks an index, a commodity or a basket of assets like an index fund, but trades like a stock on an exchange. ETFs experience price changes throughout the day as they are bought and sold.

These funds are passively managed leading to low operating expenses. Since most fund managers are trying to beat the returns of the index, if you cannot beat them, join them – buy index funds or ETFs. Index funds and ETFs can be a safer option for beginner investors to start with.

Taking Action with Long-Term Investment
When to invest: Start investing as soon as you can and benefit from compound interest.

When to sell: The longer you invest, the lower the risk – look at 5 to 10 years.

Summary – Seven Steps to Long-Term Investing
1. Get your finances in order and determine how much you can comfortably afford to invest on a monthly basis in order to benefit from compound interest

2. Determine which country, industry sector or commodity you feel will benefit from long-term growth

3. First, look for safe investments such as Fixed Income Securities like the Federal Government of Nigeria (FGN) bonds and T-bills

4. Check for good company stocks to analyse properly and invest in

5. Open an Investment Account with an investment broker, such as *Primera Africa Securities Limited*

6. Discuss your investment objectives and obtain financial advice from your financial adviser

7. Decide how you want to allocate your monthly investment – see Chapter 14 on Asset Allocation

CHAPTER 12

INVESTMENT IN STOCKS AND SHARES (SECURITIES)

The only person you are destined to become is the person you decide to be
RALPH WALDO EMERSON

There are 3,041 securities traded in the United Kingdom and 262 securities in Nigeria, talk less of other places such as Europe and the United States of America. This shows you that there is an enormous number of stocks to pick from.

Assessing which securities to invest in involves fundamental analysis, which is the examination of the financial data, management, business concept and competition of the company you are interested in.

Technical Analysis is also very important.

Fundamental Analysis of Stocks
Earnings Per Share (EPS): This is defined as the portion of a company's profit allocated to each outstanding share of common stock. EPS serves as an indicator of a company's profitability.

$$EPS = \frac{(Net\ income - Dividends\ on\ Preferred\ Stock)}{Average\ outstanding\ shares}$$

EPS is considered to be the single most important variable in determining a share's price. It is also a major component used to calculate the P/E valuation ratio.

Price to Earnings (P/E) Ratio: This looks at the relationship between the stock price and the company's earnings.

$$P/E = Stock\ price / EPS$$

In general, a high P/E suggests that investors are expecting higher earnings' growth in the future compared to companies with a lower P/E.

The following is a guide on how to interpret the P/E ratio figures quoted for the stock.
- N/A (No P/E available) – no earnings or negative earnings
- 0-10 – under-valued stock or in decline
- 10-17 – fair value stock price
- 17-25 – over-valued stock or increased earnings
- 25+ – high future growth or bubble

Investment Strategies in Stocks

Value Investing: This was started by Benjamin Graham and David Dodd, professors at Columbia Business School in 1928. It involves fundamental analysis of stocks, looking for under-valued stocks (low P/E ratios) of companies, which are performing very well. They used the concept of 'margin of safety' which is the discount of market stock price to its intrinsic value.

Warren Buffet is a famous student of Benjamin Graham.

Growth Investing – This is the investment in companies that show above average growth even if their share price is expensive (high P/E ratios). These are the dangers of buying when market has peaked.

Studies have shown that value-investing has consistently outperformed growth stocks and the market as a whole. There is a case for having both in your diversified portfolio.

Things to Look Out for When Investing in Stocks

- Major percentage (25 per cent or more) increases in current quarterly EPS
- P/E ratios – high P/E ratios for growth-investing and low P/E ratios for value-investing
- Annual EPS growth over 3 to 5 years (20 to 25 per cent).
- New highs, new products, new management as well as other indications of anticipated positive change

Cyclical Stocks

This is a stock that rises quickly when economic growth is strong and falls rapidly when growth is slowing down. An example is the automobile market; as economic growth slows, consumers have less money to spend on new cars. Another example is the housing market.

Defensive Stocks

These are also called *non-cyclical stocks*. They are stocks that tend to remain stable under difficult economic conditions. Defensive stocks include food, tobacco, oil, and utilities.

Earnings Season

These are the months in which the majority of quarterly corporate earnings are released to the public. In general, each earnings season begins one or two weeks after the last month of each quarter (December, March, June and September).

Basics of Technical Analysis

- The charts don't lie!
- Raw data might be false
- Look at the trend of the stock
- Use indicators to help with entry and exit points in the market

CHAPTER 13

BONDS AND TREASURY BILLS (FIXED INCOME SECURITIES)

**Learn from the mistakes of others. You can't live long
enough to make them all yourself.
ELEANOR ROOSEVELT**

Bonds Definition

Bonds are effectively a means through which investors lend money to a government or corporate institutions (issuer of the bond) with interest. A bond is a debt security or IOU.

Bonds are good to have as part of a diversified investment portfolio.

Investing In Bonds

Bonds have a predictable stream of payments (interest) and also repayment of the principal investment. This can help preserve and increase your capital. This is very good for retirement planning and also for other things like children's education or a new house etc.

Factors Influencing the Value of Bonds

Interest Rate: Bonds pay interest that can be fixed (most common), floating or payable at maturity. This is a percentage of the principal amount. It is a good form of investment for everyone and organisations.

- Example: 8% interest on ₦10,000 = ₦800 per year – this can be paid semi-annually i.e. ₦400 every 6 months or annually at ₦800 every year. The dollar equivalents apply to this example.

Maturity: The specific future date when the investor's principal will be repaid. This can range from 1 (one) day to 30 years. Categories of maturity are as follows:
- Short-term bonds – up to 5 years
- Intermediate bonds – 5 to 12 years
- Long-term bonds – 12+ years

Credit Quality of Bonds

Since a bond may not be redeemed or reach maturity, for a number of years and possibly decades, credit quality is another important consideration when evaluating bonds. These range from highest quality such as the US treasury bonds, which are backed by the full faith and credit of the government of the United States of America to low-grade bonds. The bond issuer is responsible for providing details of its financial soundness and credit worthiness.

Ratings Agencies

Ratings agencies assign ratings to many bonds when they are issued and monitor developments during the bond's lifetime. Their ratings are based on the in-depth analysis of the following characteristics of the bond issuer:
- Their financial condition and management
- Their economic and debt characteristics
- The specific revenue sources securing the bond

In the United States of America, there are three major rating agencies – Moody's Investor Service, Standard & Poor's Corporation (S&P) and Fitch Ratings.

The highest ratings are AAA (S&P and Fitch Ratings) and Aaa (Moody's). Bonds rated in the BBB category or higher are considered investment-grade and bonds rated BB or below are

Table of Bond Credit Quality Ratings

Credit Risk	Moody's	Standard & Poor	Fitch Ratings
Investment Grade			
Highest quality	Aaa	AAA	AAA
High quality (very strong)	Aa	AA	AA
Upper medium grade (strong)	A	A	A
Medium grade	Baa	BBB	BBB
Not Investment Grade			
Lower medium grade (somewhat speculative)	Ba	BB	BB
Low grade (speculative)	B	B	B
Poor quality -may default	Caa	CCC	CCC
Most speculative	Ca	CC	CC
No interest paid or bankruptcy petition filed	C	D	C
In default	C	D	D

Definition of a Treasury Bill (T-Bill)

The Nigerian Treasury Bill (NTB) is a short-term debt instrument issued by the Federal Government through the Central Bank of Nigeria (CBN) to provide short-term funding for the government. They are, by nature, the most liquid money market securities and they are backed by the guarantee of the Federal Government. They are usually issued for tenors of 91 days, 182 days and 364 days.

Investing In Treasury Bills (T-Bill)

Treasury Bills are discounted instruments, which are purchased for a price less than their par (face) value; and at maturity, the holder of the bills is paid the full par value by the government. Upfront interest can be re-invested to earn compounded returns.

It is a risk free investment because it carries the guarantee of the Federal Government of Nigeria.

CHAPTER 14

ASSET ALLOCATION

Risk comes from not knowing what you're doing
WARREN BUFFETT

This is the method of widening your investments across a variety of different asset sectors and geographical regions.

Asset allocation helps to reduce the chance of *all* your investments falling in worth at the same time and maximises the potential for smoother, and so, higher compound returns. This is the most efficient method in reducing risk when the assets selected rise and fall in worth independently of one another, that is, their movements in prices are not associated.

Asset allocation can effectively diversify the portfolio of an investor in one of two ways.

1. Through the addition to your portfolio of assets, which are not related to stocks and shares. As an example, adding gold, commodities, and bonds to your portfolio of shares is known as *vertical* diversification.

2. Through the addition of stocks and shares assets only from other geographical regions (such as Nigeria, the United Kingdom, the United States of America and Europe) or other sectors (such as the financial, oil and gas or retail sectors) is known as *horizontal* diversification.

Ways of Allocating Assets

1. You can strategically place your assets by allocating a fixed percentage of your capital investment to your different investments. For instance, a straightforward strategic allocation for a twenty-year term could be 50 per cent in stocks and shares, 25 per cent in bonds, 15 per cent in property and 10 per cent in commodities.

2. To exploit transient commercial or market conditions and augment returns, you can temporarily deviate from the strategic asset allocation above and revert to it when you have achieved your profits. This form of tactical asset allocation requires good knowledge of the market and good market timing.

3. The upkeep of the same portfolio weighting to each asset group, irrespective of which assets are rising or falling in value is termed the constant-weighting asset allocation. For instance, if the commodities portion rose in price from 10 per cent to 20 per cent of the portfolio, commodities would be sold and other assets purchased to revive the weighting.

When to Assess and Modify Your Portfolio of Investments

Asset allocation may need to be modified over time, for two reasons:

1. Increase in volatility of the portfolio due to rises in the value of the assets and changing market conditions. This assessment does not have to be done every day. Every 3 to 6 months is sufficient and this is the beauty of long-term investment.

2. An individual's age can lower the risk toleration of an investor, particularly in the years before retirement. The younger you are the more aggressive you can be with your investments and a large portion of your portfolio can consist of financial instruments such as equities (stocks and shares) and commodities. The closer you are to retirement age, the more cautious you should be and you might want to consider allocating a large portion of your portfolio to safer investments like bonds, treasury bills and cash.

CHAPTER 15

GETTING STARTED AND OPENING AN INVESTMENT ACCOUNT

Most people overestimate what they can do in one year and underestimate what they can do in ten years
BILL GATES

To begin your journey investing in the equities market, you need to open an investment/stockbroking account. You must always remember to check the broker's background and disciplinary history before opening an account.

Primera Africa Securities Limited, a stockbroking firm in partnership with dkbMARKETS, is a member of the Nigerian Stock Exchange and a market leader in providing equity and fixed income execution services to institutional, corporate and retail clients.

In order to open an account, you will be asked to provide personal and/or corporate information; the latter is required for institutional and corporate accounts. This information is referred to as '*Know Your Customer*' and it is a strict requirement of the regulators (the Nigerian Stock Exchange and the Securities and Exchange Commission).

The documents required are as follows:
Individuals:
- Completed application form
- Proof of employment status and occupation
- Two passport photographs (with full face forward)
- Evidence of ID i.e. international passport, driver's licence, national identity card or voter's card
- Utility (light, water or telephone) bill issued within the prior three months

Corporates:

- Completed application form
- Certificate of Incorporation of the company
- Certified true copy of Memorandum and Articles of Association of the company
- Certified true copy of form C07 (Particulars of Directors)
- Certified true copy of form C02 (Allotment of Shares)
- Two passport photographs of each signatory to the account (with full face forward)
- Identification document of signatories and directors to the account e.g. international passport, driver's licence, national identity card or voter's card
- Residence or Work Permit for foreign citizens
- Utility (light, water or telephone) bill issued within the prior three months
- Board resolution on company's letterhead paper duly signed by two directors with company seal appended

After these documents are submitted, an account will be opened and an active CSCS (Central Securities Clearing System) account will be created within two working days, at which point trading can commence.

To open an account with Primera Africa Securities Limited, do contact them at:

   Address: 24 Kofo Abayomi Street, Victoria Island, Lagos.
   Email: sales@primera-africa.com
   Telephone: +234 1 277 0827-30
   Website: www.primera-africa.com

APPENDIX

Income and Expenses Spreadsheet

	Jan-16	Feb-16	Mar-16	Apr-16	May-16	Jun-16	Jul-16	Aug-16	Sep-16	Oct-16	Nov-16	Dec-16
Income												
Salary	625,000											
Investments												
Gifts												
Total	₦625,000	₦0	₦0	₦0	₦0	₦0	₦0	₦0	₦0	₦0	₦0	₦0
Expenses												
Tithes	62,500											
Offering	2,500											
Mortgage / Rent	198,750											
School fees	62,500											
Professional subscription	20,000											
Loan 1	30,000											
Loan 2	30,000											
Mobile phone bill 1	11,250											
Mobile phone bill 2	10,000											
Gas bill	10,000											
Electricity bill	10,000											
Car Insurance	1,000											
Car Maintainance	5,000											
DSTV Subscription	2,500											
Personal Allowance Spouse 1	5,000											
Personal Allowance Spouse 2	5,000											
General Groceries	20,000											
Household Items	40,000											
Clothes & School shopping	5,000											
Charity giving	5,000											
Gifts/presents	5,000											
Holiday	12,500											
Petrol	30,000											
Entertainment	10,000											
Total	₦593,500	₦0	₦0	₦0	₦0	₦0	₦0	₦0	₦0	₦0	₦0	₦0
Balance	₦31,500	₦0	₦0	₦0	₦0	₦0	₦0	₦0	₦0	₦0	₦0	₦0

RESOURCES AND EVENTS

Coaching and Mentorship Programme
Opening a *live account* with dkbMARKETS enables you to benefit from coaching materials on forex trading, regular webinars on *live trading* and *mentorship*. Details of how to open a live account can be found on the website at www.dkbmarkets.com.

Trading and Investment 2-Day Master Classes
Attend *Live Trading and Investment* seminars and learn how to trade and invest in the financial markets. Attend this 2-day master class and benefit from in-depth teaching on the financial markets and how to profit from them.
Further details can be found at the website, www.dkbmarkets.com.

Regular Free Seminars Live and Online
dkbMARKETS also run FREE live and online seminars on trading and investing.

Social Media
Follow my forex day and swing trades by following us on twitter at www.twitter.com/dkbmarkets and "like us" on our Facebook page at www.facebook.com/dkbmarkets. You can also watch educational videos on our YouTube channel at www.youtube.com/dkbmarkets and join us on Google+ at www.google.com/+dkbMARKETSLimited